Twenty to Make

Knitted Beanies

Susie Johns

Search Press

First published in Great Britain 2012

Search Press Limited
Wellwood, North Farm Road,
Tunbridge Wells, Kent TN2 3DR

Reprint 2013 (twice)

Photographs by Debbie Patterson at
Search Press Studios
Photograph on page 47 by Rebecca Warwick
www.rebeccamayphotography.co.uk

Print ISBN: 978-1-84448-707-3
Epub ISBN: 978-1-78126-041-8
Mobi ISBN: 978-1-78126-096-8
PDF ISBN: 978-1-78126-150-7

Suppliers
If you have difficulty in obtaining any of the materials and equipment mentioned in this book, then please visit the Search Press website for details of suppliers: www.searchpress.com

Printed in China

Dedication
For my lovely children Josh, Lillie and Edith, who all look great in hats.

We would like to thank Lizzie Rampe, Shaiann and JJ Hazon, Freyja and Poppy Arthur, Ben and Sam Kersey, Polly Tracey, Dot Winter and Jett Phoenix Lucas-Winter and Florence May Warwick for featuring in this book.

Abbreviations:
alt = alternate
beg = beginning
dec = decrease
inc = increase
inc1 = increase one stitch
inc2 = increase two stitches
k = knit
m = make
m1 = make one stitch
p = purl
psso = pass slipped stitch over
rem = remaining
rep = repeat
RS = right side
sl = slip stitch
st(s) = stitch(es)
tbl = through the back loop(s)
tog = together
WS = wrong side
yfwd = yarn forward

UK and US terminology:

UK	US
cast off	bind off
stocking stitch	stockinette stitch
yarn forward	yarn over

Contents

Introduction

When it comes to keeping warm, a beanie hat is hard to beat: soft and snug, it is a great insulator that is compact enough to stuff into a pocket, ready to whip out at the slightest hint of a chill wind.

Beanies are also fun to make and an easy yet satisfying project for a beginner to tackle. A beanie hat needs only a small amount of materials, typically one or two balls of yarn, and is quick to knit, so you can create one on impulse, for yourself, or for your friends and family.

The woolly hat is currently enjoying something of a revival. Of course, the beanie means different things to different people: usually knitted, it can be snug, clinging tight to the head; it can be loose-fitting, or even slouchy; some have a brim or a ribbed band that can be rolled back; some have decorations such as a bobble, bow or buttons.

When it comes to making a fashion statement, you can really let your heart rule your head by creating a beanie to match your favourite outfit. You can try bold stripes in two or more colours – or even a whole rainbow.

You can choose to knit a beanie with a fine yarn, resulting in a thin fabric, or you can use a standard double-knitting yarn, or something more chunky: a range of yarns has been used throughout the book, to offer this choice. A natural yarn – such as merino wool, perhaps mixed with some cashmere, angora or alpaca – will provide the most warmth. Some of the patterns in this book are designed to be knitted in rows, using a pair of knitting needles, so you will need to stitch a seam or two to create your hat shape, while some are knitted in the round on a set of four double-pointed needles, giving a seamless finish.

It is important that you knit to the stated tension for each pattern because otherwise your knitting may be looser or tighter than the tension in the pattern and your hat will turn out bigger or smaller than desired, and may not fit. Most of the hats, however, are quite stretchy and versatile, and will fit a range of head sizes.

Techniques

Mattress stitch seam

This method creates an invisible seam. Working on the right side of the work, place the two edges together then, starting at the bottom edge of the work, insert a tapestry needle threaded with matching yarn under the bar between the first and second stitches on the right-hand side. Then insert the needle in the same way on the opposite edge. Repeat, working across from left to right and back again, moving up the seam like the rungs of a ladder. Do not pull the stitches tight until you reach the top of the seam, then pull the yarn ends until the two sides meet and fasten off the yarn ends securely.

Backstitch

Place the two pieces to be joined on top of one another, right sides together, then, working from right to left, one stitch in from the selvedge, bring the needle up through both layers then back down through both layers one row to the left. Bring the needle back up through both layers one row to the left, then back down one row to the right, in the same place as before. Repeat, taking the needle two rows to the left each time, and one row back.

Gathering stitch

Most of the beanie hats are worked from the bottom upwards, finishing on the top of the crown, where the last few stitches, when they are not cast off, are instead threaded on to a length of yarn and gathered together. Where the pattern requires you to do this, simply cut the working yarn, leaving a tail at least 30cm (11¾in) long, then thread this tail through the remaining stitches and pull up to gather the stitches together and close up the hole. Fasten off the yarn end securely.

Sometimes a piece of knitting is gathered to create an interesting shape – for example, on the Bow Beanie on page 40. In this case, thread a tapestry needle with matching yarn, fasten the end of the yarn to the fabric and sew a running stitch through the fabric, then pull up the yarn so that the fabric is gathered into pleats. Fasten off the yarn securely.

Making pompoms

To make a pompom, cut two circles of cardboard, each 6cm (2⅜in) in diameter and cut a 2.5cm (1in) diameter hole in the centre of each. Thread a tapestry needle with four 2m (6½ft) strands of yarn. Hold the two cardboard discs together and pass the needle through the holes, over the outside edges and back though the centre again. Continue wrapping the ring in this way until the whole ring is covered with an even layer of yarn. Using sharp scissors, cut through the yarn around the edges of the circles, inserting the tips of the blades between the two cardboard circles. Cut two 30cm (11¾in) lengths of the same yarn and insert the two strands between the cardboard layers and around the cut yarn, pulling tightly and knotting firmly to hold the bundle of short strands in place. Remove the card discs and fluff out the pompoms, then cut off any stray ends and trim to the desired size.

Buttons

When adding buttons, the yarn used for knitting the beanie may be too thick to pass through the holes in the buttons, in which case use a fine sewing needle and sewing thread.

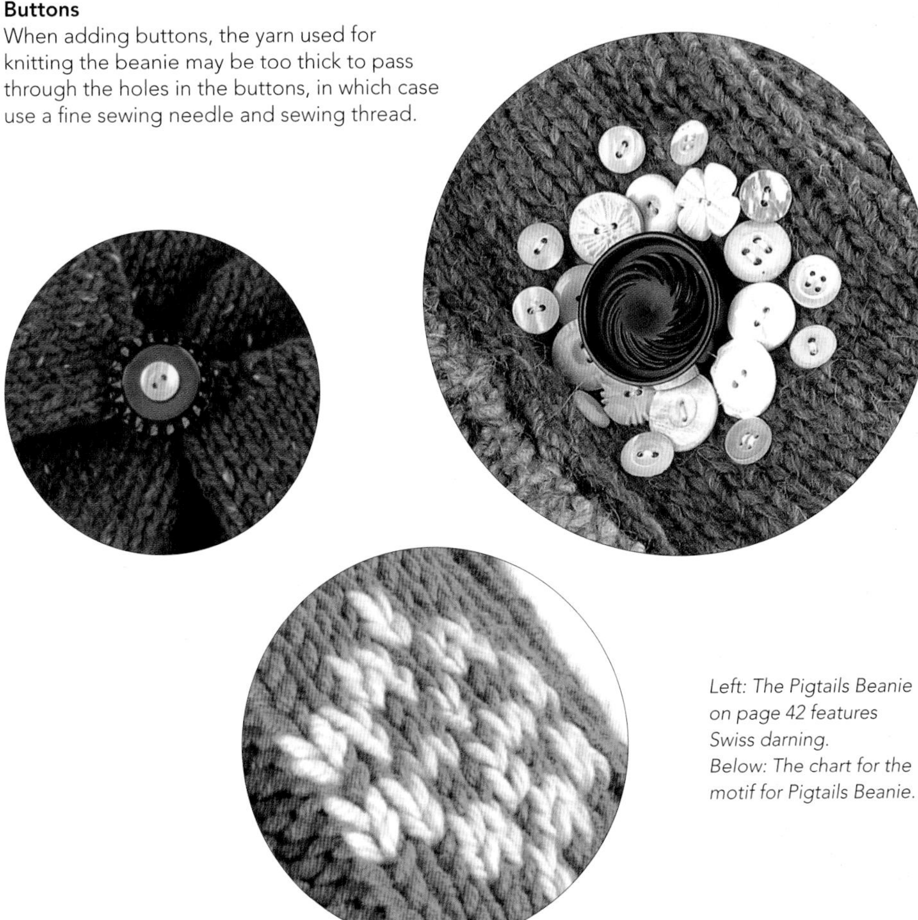

Left: The Pigtails Beanie on page 42 features Swiss darning.
Below: The chart for the motif for Pigtails Beanie.

Swiss darning

The Pigtails Beanie on page 42 has a simple motif added to the finished hat with Swiss darning, an embroidery stitch that emulates the shape of the knitted stitch and looks as though it has been knitted in.

Look closely at a row of knitting and you will see that each stitch resembles a 'V'. Thread a tapestry needle with your chosen yarn, which should, ideally, be the same weight as the yarn used for knitting, but in a contrasting colour. Secure the end to the wrong side of the fabric and bring the needle up through the point of the 'V', take it behind the two prongs of the 'V' and back down into the place where you began. Continue making stitches in this way, following the chart for positioning the stitches.

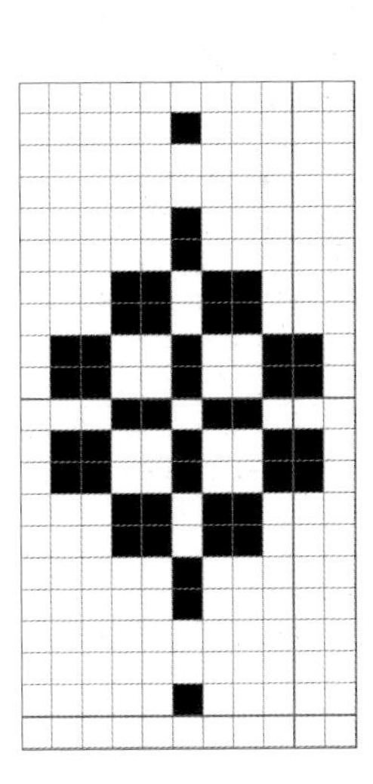

Very Easy Beanie

Materials:

2 x 50g balls aran (10-ply) yarn (100% wool) – heather

Needles:

4mm (UK 8; US 6) knitting needles

5mm (UK 6; US 8) knitting needles

Tapestry needle

Tension:

18 sts and 25 rows to 10cm (4in) measured over stocking stitch, using 5mm (UK 6; US 8) knitting needles

Measurements and sizes:

To fit an average teen or adult head

Instructions:

With 4mm needles and aran yarn, cast on 100 sts.
Row 1: (k1, p1) to end.
Rep row 1 nine times more.
Change to 5mm needles and, beg with a k row, work 46 rows in stocking stitch.
Cast off.

Making up

Stitch the seam and place at the back of the hat, then stitch the front to the back along the cast-off edge.

Simply Stylish

This hat is so easy to make, even for a beginner. For a stylish variation, choose an aran yarn with a tweedy effect (opposite). As a finishing touch, stitch the two points at the top of the hat together and finish with a decorative button – in this case a small white button on top of a larger vintage button.

Button Beanie

Materials:

2 x 50g balls aran (10-ply) yarn (wool and alpaca blend) – tweedy brown

Assorted vintage buttons – 1 large 35mm (1³⁄₈in), 10 medium 18mm (¾in), 10 small 11mm (³⁄₈in)

Sewing thread

Needles:

4.5mm (UK 7; US 7) knitting needles

Tapestry needle

Sewing needle

Tension:

15 sts and 22 rows to 10cm (4in), using 4.5mm (UK 7; US 7) knitting needles and aran yarn, measured over stocking stitch.

Measurements and sizes:

To fit an average female adult head

Instructions:

Band

Using 4.5mm needles and aran yarn, cast on 13 sts.
Beg with a purl row, work 101 rows in stocking stitch (1 row purl, 1 row plain).
Cast off.

Crown

Using 4.5mm needles and aran yarn, cast on 6 sts.
Row 1: inc1, k4, inc1 (8 sts).
Row 2: inc1, k6, inc1 (10 sts).
Row 3: inc1, k8, inc1 (12 sts).
Row 4: inc1, k10, inc1 (14 sts).
Row 5: knit.
Row 6: inc1, k to last st, inc1.
Rep rows 5 and 6 twice more (20 sts).
Knit 12 rows.
Row 23: k2tog, k to last 2 sts, k2tog.
Row 24: knit.
Rep rows 23 and 24 twice more.
Row 29: k2tog, k to last 2 sts, k2tog.
Rep row 29 three times (6 sts). Cast off.

Brim

Using 4.5mm needles and aran yarn, cast on 18 sts.
Rows 1–4: knit.
Row 5: k15; turn.
Row 6: knit.
Rep rows 1–6 until shorter edge of the brim is the same length as the band.
Cast off.

Making up

Stitch the cast-on and cast-off edges of the band together to form a ring, then stitch one edge to the crown. Pin the right side of the brim to the wrong side of the band, easing it slightly to fit, then stitch it in place. Fold the brim in half, attaching the edge to the seam at intervals, to hold it in place.

Stitch the large button to the band, on the side opposite the seam, placing it centrally, then stitch the medium buttons in a circle around the large button, and the small buttons around the edges.

Cute as a Button

When working short rows (as on the brim), for a neat finish, knit the number of stitches stated then, before turning, bring the yarn to the front of your work, slip the next stitch purlwise, take the yarn back and slip the stitch back on to the left-hand needle.

Beret Beanie

Materials:

2 x 50g balls double-knitting (8-ply) yarn (100% alpaca) – violet

Needles:

3.25mm (UK 10; US 3) knitting needles

3.75mm (UK 9; US 5) knitting needles

Tapestry needle

Tension:

23 sts and 28 rows to 10cm (4in), using 3.75mm (UK 9; US 5) knitting needles, measured over stocking stitch.

Measurements and sizes:

To fit an average female adult head

Instructions:

Band

Using 3.25mm needles and alpaca yarn, cast on 122 sts.
Row 1: (k1, p1) to end.
Rep row 1 thirteen times.
Row 15: k1 *yfwd, k2tog, rep from * to last st, k1
Rep row 1 thirteen times.
Row 29: k2, (m1, k3) 12 times, (m1, k2) 24 times, (m1, k3) 12 times (170 sts).
Row 30: purl.

Change to 3.75mm needles and, beg with a k row, work in stocking stitch for 24 rows.
Row 55: (k15, k2tog) 10 times (160 sts).
Row 56 and each even-numbered row: purl.
Row 57: (k14, k2tog) 10 times (150 sts).
Row 59: (k13, k2tog) 10 times (140 sts).
Row 61: (k12, k2tog) 10 times (130 sts).
Row 63: (k11, k2tog) 10 times (120 sts).
Row 65: (k10, k2tog) 10 times (110 sts).
Row 67: (k9, k2tog) 10 times (100 sts).
Row 69: (k8, k2tog) 10 times (90 sts).
Row 71: (k7, k2tog) 10 times (80 sts).
Row 73: (k6, k2tog) 10 times (70 sts).
Row 75: (k5, k2tog) 10 times (60 sts).
Row 77: (k4, k2tog) 10 times (50 sts).
Row 79: (k3, k2tog) 10 times (40 sts).
Row 81: (k2, k2tog) 10 times (30 sts).
Row 83: (k1, k2tog) 10 times (20 sts).
Row 85: (k2tog) 10 times (10 sts).
Row 80: (p2tog) 5 times (5 sts).
Beg with a k row, work 10 rows in stocking stitch.
Cast off and cut yarn, leaving a long tail.

Making up

Fold the ribbed band to the inside along the eyelet row and stitch the cast-on edge to the top of the ribbing. With right sides together and using the tail of yarn, stitch the back seam, including the stalk at the centre of the crown, in backstitch; turn right sides out.

Violet Twist

There is an eyelet row in the centre of the ribbed band which, when the band is folded in half, creates a soft band of double thickness with a picot edge.

Blossom Beanie

Materials:

2 x 50g balls double-knitting (8-ply) yarn (100% acrylic) – ivory

Large button 35mm ($1^{3}/_{8}$in)

Needles:

3.75mm (UK 9; US 5) knitting needles

Tapestry needle

Tension:

22 sts and 30 rows to 10cm (4in) measured over stocking stitch

Measurements and sizes:

To fit an average female adult head

Instructions:

Ribbed band

Using 3.75mm needles and ivory double-knitting yarn, cast on 22 sts.
Row 1: sl1, (k2, p2) 5 times, k1.
Rep row 1 167 times; cast off in pattern; do not cut yarn but pick up and knit 78 sts along long edge (including st already on needle).

Crown

Row 1: inc1 in each st (156 sts).
Row 2: purl.
Row 3: (k12, inc1) 12 times (168 sts).
Beg with a p row, work 22 rows in stocking stitch.
Row 26: (k12, k2tog) 12 times (156 sts).
Row 27 and each odd-numbered (WS) row: purl.
Row 28: (k11, k2tog) 12 times (144 sts).
Row 30: (k10, k2tog) 12 times (132 sts).
Row 32: (k9, k2tog) 12 times (120 sts).
Row 34: (k8, k2tog) 12 times (108 sts).
Row 36: (k7, k2tog) 12 times (96 sts).
Row 38: (k6, k2tog) 12 times (84 sts).
Row 40: (k5, k2tog) 12 times (72 sts).
Row 42: (k4, k2tog) 12 times (60 sts).
Row 44: (k3, k2tog) 12 times (48 sts).
Row 46: (k2, k2tog) 12 times (36 sts).
Row 48: (k1, k2tog) 12 times (24 sts).
Row 49: (p2tog) 12 times (12 sts).
Row 50: (k2tog) 6 times.
Cut yarn, leaving a long tail, and thread through rem 6 sts.

Flower petals (make 5)

Using 3.75mm needles and double-knitting yarn, cast on 5 sts.
Row 1: inc in each st to end (10 sts).
Row 2: purl.
Row 3: inc in each st to end (20 sts).
Row 4: purl.
Row 5: inc in each st to end (40 sts).
Beg with a purl row, work 3 rows in stocking stitch.
Cast off; cut yarn and fasten off.

Centre

Using 3.75mm needles and double-knitting yarn, cast on 5 sts.
Row 1: inc in each st to end (10 sts).
Row 2: purl.
Row 3: inc in each st to end (20 sts).
Beg with a purl row, work 3 rows in stocking stitch.
Cut yarn and thread through all sts.

Making up

Stitch the cast-on and cast-off rows of the ribbed band together using a running stitch, then pull up to gather and fasten off. With right sides facing, join the seam on to the crown with mattress stitch.

Join the straight edges of each petal using a running stitch, then pull up very slightly to flatten the centre of the petal. Stitch the five petals in place, overlapping, across the gathered join on the ribbed band. Join the seam on the flower centre, then run a gathering stitch around the edge of the circle. Place a large button on the wrong side and pull up the tail of yarn to gather around the button, then stitch the flower centre firmly in place in the middle of the five petals.

Vintage Petals

The past continues to have an influence on today's fashions and this hat, in a style that flatters most face shapes, evokes the classic elegance of a bygone era. The pull-on cloche – the French word for 'bell' – became the must-have fashion accessory in the 1920s: a head-hugging style designed to be worn low on the forehead. Embellished with a five-petalled flower, this version has a wide horizontal band and slightly slouchy styling, which makes it comfortable to wear.

Charm Beanie

Materials:

2 x 50g balls double-knitting (8-ply) yarn (merino wool and cashmere blend) – pink

Phone charm loop attachment

1 x 10mm split ring

6 x 6mm split rings

6 small flower charms

Needles:

3.25mm (UK 10; US 3) knitting needles

4mm (UK 8; US 6) knitting needles

Tapestry needle

Tension:

22 sts and 30 rows to 10cm (4in), using 3.25mm (UK 10; US 3) knitting needles, measured over stocking stitch.

Measurements and sizes:

To fit a child aged 3–6 years

Instructions:

Using 3.25mm needles and double-knitting yarn, cast on 84 sts.
Row 1: (k1, p1) to end.
Rep row 1 five times more.
Change to 4mm needles.
Row 7: (k3, m1) 28 times (112 sts).
Beg with a p row, work 7 rows in stocking stitch.
Row 15: (k8, m1) 14 times (126 sts).
Beg with a p row, work 21 rows in stocking stitch.
Row 37: (k7, k2tog) 14 times (112 stitches).
Beg with a p row, work 5 rows in stocking stitch.
Row 43: (k13, k3tog) 7 times (98 sts).
Beg with a p row, work 5 rows in stocking stitch.
Row 49: (k11, k3tog) 7 times (84 sts).
Beg with a p row, work 3 rows in stocking stitch.
Row 53: (k9, k3tog) 7 times (70 sts).
Beg with a p row, work 3 rows in stocking stitch.
Row 57: (k7, k3tog) 7 times (56 sts).
Beg with a p row, work 3 rows in stocking stitch.
Row 61: (k5, k3tog) 7 times (42 sts).
Beg with a p row, work 3 rows in stocking stitch.
Row 65: (k3, k3tog) 7 times (28 sts).
Row 66: purl.
Row 67: (k1, k3tog) 7 times (14 sts).
Row 68: (p2tog) 7 times.
Cut yarn and thread tail through rem 7 sts.

Making up

Pull up the tail of yarn to gather the stitches together at the centre of the crown. Thread the tail through the loop on the phone charm attachment then, with right sides together and using the tail of yarn, stitch the back seam in backstitch; turn right sides out.

Attach a split ring to the ring on the phone charm attachment, then attach the small flower charms using the smaller split rings.

Princess Charming

A beret is comfortable to wear and suits most head shapes. The little charms add a personal touch – and if you attach them with a split ring, they can easily be removed and replaced with different ones.

Beastie Beanie

Materials:

1 50g ball double-knitting (8-ply) yarn (100% wool) – red

1 50g ball double-knitting (8-ply) yarn (100% wool) – orange

Small amounts of double-knitting (8-ply) yarn white, apple green, turquoise, black

Polyester toy stuffing

2 large 35mm (1⅜in) 4-hole buttons – green

Needles:

4.5mm (UK 7; US 7) knitting needles

3.75mm (UK 9; US 5) knitting needles

Tapestry needle

Tension:

18 sts and 25 rows to 10cm (4in) measured over stocking stitch, using 4.5mm (UK 7; US 7) knitting needles

Measurement and sizes:

To fit an average adult head

Instructions:

Hat

With 4.5mm needles and red double-knitting yarn, cast on 80 sts.
Beg with a knit row, work 62 rows in stocking stitch (1 row knit, 1 row purl).
Cast off.

Eye patch (make 2)

Using 3.75mm needles and apple green double-knitting yarn, cast on 8 sts.
Rows 1 and 2: knit.
Row 3: inc1, k to last st, inc1.
Row 4 and 5: sl1, k to end.
Rep rows 3–5 twice more (14 sts).
Rows 12 and 13: sl1, k to end.
Row 14: k2tog, k to last 2 sts, k2tog.
Rows 15 and 16: sl1, k to end.
Rep rows 14–16 once more (10 sts).
Row 20: sl1, k to end.
Row 21: k2tog, k4, k2 tog.
Cast off rem 8 sts.

Mouth

Using 3.75mm needles and orange double-knitting yarn, cast on 42 sts.
Row 1: (k6, inc1 in the next st) 6 times (48 sts).
Row 2 and all even-numbered rows: purl.
Row 3: (k7, inc1 in the next st) 6 times (54 sts).
Row 5: (k8, inc1 in the next st) 6 times (60 sts).
Row 7: (k9, inc1 in the next st) 6 times (66 sts).
Beg with a purl row, work 3 rows in stocking stitch.
Row 11: (k9, k2tog) 6 times (60 sts).
Row 13: (k8, k2tog) 6 times (54 sts).
Row 15: (k7, k2tog) 6 times (48 sts).
Row 17: (k6, k2tog) 6 times (42 sts).
Cast off.

Teeth

Using 3.75mm needles and white double-knitting yarn, cast on 18 sts.
Row 1: knit
Row 2: inc1, k to last st, inc1.
Rep rows 1 and 2 once more (22 sts).
Knit 5 rows.
Row 10: k2tog, k to last 2 sts, k2tog.
Row 11: knit.
Rep rows 10 and 11 once more (18 sts).
Cast off.

Making up

Stitch the seam and place at the back of the hat, then stitch the front to the back along the cast-off edge. Stitch the teeth in place on the lower half of the front, then stitch on the black lines. For the mouth, stitch the ends to form a ring, then oversew the cast-on and cast-off edges together, adding stuffing to pad out the shape. Stitch it in place, over the edges of the teeth. Stitch the eye patches in place, then add a button on top of each, using white yarn. Make two pompoms from turquoise yarn and stitch one to each corner of the hat.

Monster Knit

The fun starts here: create your own beast by using different colours from your yarn stash and customising the features. For a more conventional hat, you can,of course choose not to add the eyes and mouth.

Panda Beanie

Materials:

2 x 50g balls aran (10-ply) yarn (wool and cashmere blend) – cream

1 50g ball of double-knitting (8-ply) yarn (100%) wool – black

2 sew-on googly eyes

Needles and tools:

4mm (UK 8; US 6) knitting needles

5mm (UK 6; US 8) knitting needles

Stitch holder

Tapestry needle

Tension:

18 sts and 26 rows to 10cm (4in), using 5mm (UK 6; US 8) knitting needles and aran (10-ply) yarn, measured over stocking stitch.

Measurements and sizes:

To fit an average adult head

Instructions:

Hat

Using 4mm needles and cream aran yarn, cast on 108 sts.
Row 1: (k1, p1) to end.
Rep row 1 seven times.
Change to 5mm needles and, beg with a knit row, work 34 rows in stocking stitch.
*Row 43: k1, sl1, k1, psso, k48, k2tog, k1, turn and leave rem sts on a holder.
Row 44: purl.
Row 45: knit.
Row 46: purl.
Row 47: k1, sl1, k1, psso, k to last 3 sts, k2tog, k1.
Row 48: purl.
Rep rows 47 and 48 until 44 sts rem.
Next row: k1, sl1, k2tog, psso, k to last 4 sts, k3tog, k1.
Next row: purl.
Rep last 2 rows 3 times more (28 sts).
Next row: k1, sl1, k2tog, psso, (k2tog) 10 times, k3tog, k1 (14 sts).
Cast off purlwise.

Rejoin yarn to sts on holder and rep from * to end.

Ear (make 2)

Note that yarn is used double.
Using 5mm needles and two strands of black double-knitting yarn, cast on 16 sts.
Row 1: k each st tbl.
Rep row 1 eleven times more.
Row 13: k1, sl1, k1, psso, k each st tbl to last 3 sts, k2tog, k1.
Row 14: k each st tbl.
Rows 15 and 16: as rows 13 and 14.
Rows 17, 18 and 19: as row 13.
Cast off rem 6 sts.
Cast off and cut yarn, leaving a long tail.

Eye patch (make 2)

Using 4mm needles and black double-knitting yarn, cast on 8 sts.
Row 1: knit.
Row 2: inc1, k to last st, inc1.
Row 3–5: sl1, k to end.
Rep rows 2–5 twice more (14 sts).
Rows 14–20: sl1, k to end.
Row 21: k2tog, k to last 2 sts, k2tog.
Rows 22–24: sl1, k to end.
Rep rows 21–24 once more (10 sts).
Row 29: sl1, k to end.
Row 30: k2tog, k4, k2 tog.
Cast off rem 8 sts.

Nose

Using 4mm needles and black double-knitting yarn, cast on 1 st.
Row 1: inc2 by knitting into front, back and front of st (3 sts).
Rows 2 and 3: sl1, k to end.
Row 4: inc1, k1, inc1 (5 sts).
Rows 5 and 6: sl1, k to end.
Row 7: inc1, k to last st, inc1.
Rep rows 5–7 twice more (11 sts).
Rows 14–18: sl1, k to end.
Cast off.

Making up

With right sides together and using the tail of yarn, stitch the side seam in backstitch. Neaten the ears, using the tails of yarn, then insert the straight edge of the ear into the centre of the sloping edge at each side. Pin it in place, then stitch the seam, trapping the ear between the layers. Turn right sides out. Stitch the eye patches in place on the front of the hat and stitch on the googly eyes. Stitch the nose in place, with the lower point at the top of the ribbed band. Add a small line of stitches below the nose.

Rolled Up Beanie

Materials:

2 x 50g balls double-knitting (8-ply) yarn (mohair blend) – pink

Needles:

2 pairs 4mm (UK 8; US 6) double-pointed knitting needles

Tapestry needle

Tension:

20 sts and 28 rows to 10cm (4in) measured over stocking stitch

Measurements and sizes:

To fit a medium-large female adult head

Instructions:

Using two pairs of 4mm double-pointed needles and mohair yarn, cast on 108 sts and divide these sts between three of the needles, using the fourth to knit.
Knit 44 rounds.
Round 45: (k10, k2tog) 9 times (99 sts).
Round 46: (k9, k2tog) 9 times (90 sts).
Round 47: (k8, k2tog) 9 times (81 sts).
Round 48: (k7, k2tog) 9 times (72 sts).
Round 49: (k6, k2tog) 9 times (63 sts).
Round 50: (k5, k2tog) 9 times (54 sts).
Round 51: (k4, k2tog) 9 times (45 sts).
Round 52: (k3, k2tog) 9 times (36 sts).
Round 53: (k2, k2tog) 9 times (27 sts).
Round 54: (k1, k2tog) 9 times (18 sts).
Round 55: (k2tog) 9 times (9 sts).
Row 56: (k3tog) 3 times (3 sts).
Transfer the rem 3 sts on to one needle and continue with two needles as follows:
Row 57: k3; do not turn but slide sts to other end of needle. Rep row 57 nine times more; cast off.

Making up
Weave in the tails of yarn neatly.

Sweet as Candy

For a child-size version, use 4-ply (fingering) yarn and 3mm (UK 11, US 3) needles, and follow the same pattern. For a beanie without the stalk on top, follow the pattern to the end of round 55, then cut the yarn, leaving a tail, thread the tail through the remaining 9 sts, pull up to close the gap and fasten off securely.

Long, Cool Beanie

Materials:

2 x 50g balls double-knitting (8-ply) yarn (100% wool) – red

Needles:

3.25mm (UK 10; US 3) knitting needles

Tapestry needle

Tension:

32 sts and 30 rows to 10cm (4in) measured over single rib (measured without stretching)

Measurements and sizes:

To fit an average adult head

Instructions:

With 3.25mm needles and double-knitting yarn, cast on 128 sts.
Row 1: (k1, p1) to end.
Rep row 1 61 times more (until work measures approximately 21cm).
Row 63: *sl1 knitwise, k2tog, psso, (k1, p1) 6 times, k1, rep from * seven times more (112 sts).
Row 64 (and every even-numbered row): (k1, p1) to end of row.
Row 65: *sl1 knitwise, k2tog, psso, (k1, p1) 5 times, k1, rep from * to end (96 sts).
Row 67: *sl1 knitwise, k2tog, psso, (k1, p1) 4 times, k1, rep from * to end (80 sts).
Row 69: *sl1 knitwise, k2tog, psso, (k1, p1) 3 times, k1, rep from * to end (64 sts).
Row 71: *sl1 knitwise, k2tog, psso, (k1, p1) twice, k1, rep from * to end (48 sts).
Row 73: *sl1 knitwise, k2tog, psso, k1, p1, k1, rep from * to end (32 sts).
Row 74: (p2tog) 16 times (16 sts).
Row 75: (k2tog) 8 times.
Cut yarn and thread through rem 8 sts.

Making up

Stitch back seam.

Cosy Cool

This hat is ideal for anyone who prefers understated style. The ribbing stretches to accommodate a range of head sizes and the hat is versatile: it can be worn slouchy or rolled up to form a neat brim.

Pompom Beanie

Materials:

1 50g ball 4-ply (fingering) yarn (100% wool or wool blend) – violet (A)

1 50g ball 4-ply (fingering) yarn (100% wool or wool blend) – lavender (B)

1 50g ball mohair yarn – orange

Needles:

2.75mm (UK 12; US 2) knitting needles

3.25mm (UK 10; US 3) knitting needles

Tapestry needle

2.75mm (US 2) crochet hook

Tension:

28 sts and 36 rows to 10cm (4in), using 3.25mm (UK 10; US 3) knitting needles, measured over stocking stitch

Measurements and sizes:

To fit an average adult head

Instructions:

Hat

Using 2.75mm needles and yarn A, cast on 122 sts.
Row 1: (k1, p1) to end, k1.
Rep row 1 five times.
Do not cut yarn A but join in yarn B and change to 3.25mm needles.
Row 7: k2, (m1, k3) 12 times, (m1, k2) 24 times, (m1, k3) 12 times (170 sts).
Row 8: purl.
Beg with a k row, work in stocking stitch for 2 rows; do not cut yarn B but pick up yarn A.
Beg with a k row, work in stocking stitch for 4 rows; do not cut yarn B but pick up yarn A.
Continue in this way, working in 4-row stripes, alternating the two colours, until you have worked a total of 15 stripes (not counting rib band).
Row 67: (k15, k2tog) 10 times (160 sts).
Row 68 (and all even-numbered rows): purl.
Row 69: (k14, k2tog) 10 times (150 sts).
Row 71: (k13, k2tog) 10 times (140 sts).
Row 73: (k12, k2tog) 10 times (130 sts).
Row 75: (k11, k2tog) 10 times (120 sts).
Row 77: (k10, k2tog) 10 times (110 sts).
Row 79: (k9, k2tog) 10 times (100 sts).
Row 81: (k8, k2tog) 10 times (90 sts).
Row 83: (k7, k2tog) 10 times (80 sts).
Row 85: (k6, k2tog) 10 times (70 sts).
Row 87: (k5, k2tog) 10 times (60 sts).
Row 89: (k4, k2tog) 10 times (50 sts).
Row 91: (k3, k2tog) 10 times (40 sts).
Row 93: (k2, k2tog) 10 times (30 sts).
Row 95: (k1, k2tog) 10 times (20 sts).
Row 97: (k2tog) 10 times.
Cut yarn and thread tail through rem 10 sts.

Pompoms

Using orange mohair yarn, make 6 pompoms following the instructions on page 6, and trim them with scissors to make them smaller.

Cords

Using a 2.75mm (US 2) crochet hook and yarn A, make three chains; one 60ch, one 70ch, one 80ch.

Making up

Pull up the tail of yarn at the crown and secure it with a few stitches. With right sides together and using the tails of yarn, stitch the back seam in backstitch; turn right sides out. Stitch the centre of each cord to the top of the hat, then attach a pompom to each of the six ends.

Snug and Stripey

You don't have to make a purple hat: the subtle effect of the stripes can be achieved with any two closely-matched shades of your chosen colour. You will need a 50g ball of each.

Big Beret Beanie

Materials:

2 x 50g balls self-striping double-knitting (8-ply) yarn – multicoloured

Needles:

3.25mm (UK 10; US 3) knitting needles

4mm (UK 8; US 6) knitting needles

Tapestry needle

Tension

22 sts and 30 rows to 10cm (4in), using 4mm (UK 8; US 6) knitting needles, measured over stocking stitch

Measurements and sizes

To fit an average female adult head

Instructions:

Hat

Using 3.25mm needles and double-knitting yarn, cast on 115 sts.
Row 1: k1, *p1, k1; rep from * to end.
Row 2: p1, *k1, p1; rep from * to end.
Rep rows 1 and 2 four times more, then row 1 once more.
Row 12: p1, *inc1 knitwise, p1, inc1 knitwise, p1, k1, inc1 purlwise, k1, inc1 purlwise, k1, p1; rep from * to last 4 sts, (inc1, p1) twice (161 sts).
Change to 4mm needles.

Main part

Row 1 (RS): knit.
Row 2: purl.
Row 3: k1, *m1, k19, m1, k1; rep from * to end (177 sts).
Beg with a p row, work 3 rows in stocking stitch.
Row 7: k1, *m1, k21, m1, k1; rep from * to end (193 sts).
Beg with a p row, work 3 rows in stocking stitch.
Row 11: k1, *m1, k23, m1, k1; rep from * to end (209 sts).
Beg with a p row, work 3 rows in stocking stitch.
Row 15: k1, m1, k25, m1, k1; rep from * to end (225 sts).
Beg with a p row, work 3 rows in stocking stitch.
Row 19: k1, *m1, k27, m1, k1; rep from * to end (241 sts).
Beg with a p row, work 3 rows in stocking stitch.
Row 23: k1, *k2tog, k25, sl1, k1, psso, k1; rep from * to end (225 sts).
Beg with a p row, work 3 rows in stocking stitch.
Row 27: k1, k2tog, k23, sl1, k1, psso, k1; rep from * to end (209 sts).
Beg with a p row, work 3 rows in stocking stitch.
Row 31: k1, k2tog, k21, sl1, k1, psso, k1; rep from * to end (193 sts).
Beg with a p row, work 3 rows in stocking stitch.
Row 35: k1, k2tog, k19, sl1, k1, psso, k1; rep from * to end (177 sts).
Beg with a p row, work 3 rows in stocking stitch.
Row 39: k1, k2tog, k17, sl1, k1, psso, k1; rep from * to end (161 sts).
Beg with a p row, work 3 rows in stocking stitch.
Row 43: k1, k2tog, k15, sl1, k1, psso, k1; rep from * to end (145 sts).
Beg with a p row, work 3 rows in stocking stitch.
Row 47: k1, k2tog, k13, sl1, k1, psso, k1; rep from * to end (129 sts).
Beg with a p row, work 3 rows in stocking stitch.
Row 51: k2tog, k13, *sl2, k1, p2sso, k13; rep from * to end (113 sts).
Row 52: purl.
Row 53: k1, *k2tog, k9, k2tog, k1; rep from * to end (97 sts).

Row 54: purl.
Row 55: k1, *k1, k2tog, k4, sl1, k1, psso, k3; rep from * to end (81 sts).
Row 56: p1, *p2, p2tog tbl, p1, p2tog, p3; rep from * to end (65 sts).
Row 57: k1, *k1, k2tog, k1, sl1, k1, psso, k2; rep from * to end (49 sts).
Row 58: p1, *p1, sl2 purlwise tbl, p1, p2sso, p2; rep from * to end (33 sts).
Row 59: k1, *sl2tog, k1, p2sso, k1; rep from * to end.
Cut yarn and thread tail through rem 17 sts.

Making up

With right sides together, stitch up the back seam in backstitch; turn right sides out.

Flower Power Beanie

Materials:

2 x 50g balls double-knitting (8-ply) yarn (100% wool or wool blend) – damson

Small amounts of double-knitting (8-ply) yarn – dusty pink and apricot

2 x 29mm (1¼in) buttons

Small amount of polyester toy stuffing

Needles:

3.75mm (UK 9; US 5) knitting needles

Tapestry needle

Tension:

15 sts and 25 rows to 10cm (4in) measured over single rib, using 3.75mm (UK 9; US 5) knitting needles (measured without stretching)

Measurements and sizes:

To fit an average female adult head

Instructions:

Hat

With 3.75mm needles and damson double-knitting yarn, cast on 112 sts.
Row 1: (k1, p1) to end.
Rep row 1 35 times more.
Row 37: *sl1 knitwise, k2tog, psso, (k1, p1) 5 times, k1, rep from * to end (96 sts).
Row 38 (and every even-numbered row): (k1, p1) to end of row.
Row 39: *sl1 knitwise, k2tog, psso, (k1, p1) 4 times, k1, rep from * to end (80 sts).
Row 41: *sl1 knitwise, k2tog, psso, (k1, p1) 3 times, k1, rep from * to end (64 sts).
Row 43: *sl1 knitwise, k2tog, psso, (k1, p1) twice, k1, rep from * to end (48 sts).
Row 45: *sl1 knitwise, k2tog, psso, k1, p1, k1, rep from * to end (32 sts).
Row 47: (k2tog) 16 times (16 sts).
Row 49: (k2tog) 8 times.
Cut yarn and thread through rem 8 sts.

Pink Flower

Petals (made in one piece)
With 3.75mm needles and dusky pink double-knitting yarn, cast on 11 sts.
Row 1: knit 1 row tbl.
Row 2: k to end.
Row 3: inc 1, k to end (12 sts).
Knit 3 rows.
Row 7: k2tog, k to end (11 sts).
Row 8: k to end.
Row 9: cast off 9, k rem st.
Row 10: k2, cast on 9 (11 sts).
Rep rows 1 to 10 four times, then rows 1 to 8 once; cast off.

Centre

With 3.75mm needles and apricot double-knitting yarn, cast on 2 sts.
Row 1: inc1, k to end.
Rep row 1 until there are 6 sts.
Knit 3 rows.
Next row: cast off 1, k to end.
Rep last row until there are 2 sts.
Cast off; break yarn and fasten off.
Make a second flower, reversing the colours.

Making up

Pull up the tail of yarn to gather the stitches on the final row and secure then, with right sides together and using the tail of yarn, stitch the back seam.

To make each flower, bring the two edges of the petals together to make a circle of petals and stitch the lower corners of the two ends together; run a gathering stitch around the centre, along the base of each petal and pull it up tightly to gather. Run a gathering stitch around the edge of the centre, place a tiny wad of polyester stuffing inside and a 29mm (1¼in) button on top of the stuffing, then pull it tightly to gather up and enclose the button. Stitch the flower centre firmly in place in the centre of the petals, then stitch it in place on the hat.

Blooming Lovely!

The directions opposite are for an adult-size hat. To make a child-size version, follow the same pattern but use 4-ply (fingering) yarn and 3mm (UK 11, US 3) knitting needles.

Slouch Beanie

Materials:

2 x 50g balls aran (10-ply) yarn (merino and cashmere blend) – plum

Needles:

4mm (UK 8; US 6) knitting needles

5mm (UK 6; US 8) knitting needles

Tapestry needle

Tension:

18 sts and 26 rows to 10cm (4in), using 5mm (UK 6; US 8) knitting needles, measured over stocking stitch.

Measurements and sizes:

To fit an average adult head

Instructions:

Using 4mm needles and aran yarn, cast on 90 sts.
Row 1: (k1, p1) to end.
Rep row 1 nine times more.
Change to 5mm needles.
Beg with a knit row, work 50 rows in stocking stitch (1 row knit, 1 row purl).
Row 61: (k13, k2tog) 6 times (84 sts).
Row 62 and every even-numbered row: purl.
Row 63: (k12, k2tog) 6 times (78 sts).
Row 65: (k11, k2tog) 6 times (72 sts).
Row 67: (k10, k2tog) 6 times (66 sts).
Row 69: (k9, k2tog) 6 times (60 sts).
Row 71: (k8, k2tog) 6 times (54 sts).
Row 73: (k7, k2tog) 6 times (48 sts).
Row 75: (k6, k2tog) 6 times (42 sts).
Row 77: (k5, k2tog) 6 times (36 sts).
Row 79: (k4, k2tog) 6 times (30 sts).
Row 81: (k3, k2tog) 6 times (24 sts).
Row 83: (k2tog) 12 times.
Cut yarn and thread tail through rem 12 sts.

Making up

Pull up the tail of yarn to gather the stitches on the final row and secure, then with right sides together and using the tail of yarn, stitch up the back seam.

Relaxed Style

This is a very simple beanie that will flatter most head shapes and suits both men and women.

Rainbow Beanie

Materials:

Approx 10–15g 4-ply (fingering) yarn (10
wool) in each of the following colours
pale blue, turquoise, pale green, yellc
orange, red, pink, plum and violet

Needles:

2.75mm (UK 12; US 2) knitting needles

3.25mm (UK 10; US 3) knitting needles

Tapestry needle

Tension:

28 sts and 36 rows to 10cm (4in), using 3.25mm (UK 10; US 3) knitting needles, measured over stocking stitch.

Measurements and sizes:

To fit a child aged 5–young teen

Instructions:

Using 2.75mm needles and blue yarn, ca
on 126 sts.
Row 1: (k1, p1) to end, k1.
Rep row 1 five times.
Row 7: * k3, m1, rep from * to last 3 sts, k3 (168 sts).
Row 8: purl.
Change to 3.25mm needles and pale blue.
Beg with a k row, work in stocking stitch for 6 rows; cut pale blue and join in turquoise.
Beg with a k row, work in stocking stitch for 6 rows; cut turquoise and join in pale green.
Beg with a k row, work in stocking stitch for 6 rows; cut pale green and join in yellow.
Beg with a k row, work in stocking stitch for 6 rows; cut yellow and join in orange.
Beg with a k row, work in stocking stitch for 6 rows; cut orange and join in red.
Beg with a k row, work in stocking stitch for 6 rows; cut red and join in pink.
Beg with a k row, work in stocking stitch for 6 rows; cut pink and join in plum.
Beg with a k row, work 4 rows in stocking stitch.
Row 55: (k12, k2tog) 12 times (156 sts).
Row 56 and each even-numbered row: purl.
Row 57: (k11, k2tog) 12 times (144 sts).
Row 58: using violet, (k10, k2tog) 12 times (132 sts).
Row 59: (k9, k2tog) 12 times (120 sts).
Row 60: (k8, k2tog) 12 times (108 sts).
Row 61: using blue, (k7, k2tog) 12 times (96 sts).
Row 62: (k6, k2tog) 12 times (84 sts).
Row 63: (k5, k2tog) 12 times (72 sts).
Row 64: using pale blue, (k4, k2tog) 12 times (60 sts).
Row 65: (k3, k2tog) 12 times (48 sts).
Row 66: (k2, k2tog) 12 times (36 sts).
Row 67: using turquoise, (k1, k2tog) 12 times (24 sts).
Row 68: (k2tog) 12 times (12 sts).
Row 69: (p2tog) 6 times.
Cut yarn and thread tail through rem 6 sts.

Pompom

Using spare yarn in several colours, make a pompom following the instructions on page 6.

Making up

Pull up the tail of yarn at the crown and secure with a few stitches. With right sides together and using the tails of yarn, stitch up the back seam in backstitch; turn right sides out. Use any leftover yarn to make a multicoloured pompom and stitch it to the centre of the crown.

Hat of Many Colours

For an adult version, follow the same pattern but use 8-ply (double-knitting) yarn, with 3.25mm (UK 10, US 3) needles for the ribbed band and 4mm (UK 8, US 6) needles for the main part of the hat. If you don't want a whole spectrum of colours, just choose two – you'll need one 50g ball of each.

Lacy Beanie

Materials:

2 x 50g balls double-knitting (8-ply) yarn (100% wool or wool blend) – turquoise blue

Needles:

Five 3.25mm (UK 10; US 3) double-pointed knitting needles

Tapestry needle

Tension:

24 sts and 28 rows to 10cm (4in), using 3.25mm (UK 10; US 3) knitting needles, measured over stocking stitch.

Measurements and sizes:

To fit a small–medium female adult head

Instructions:

Using five 3.25mm needles and double-knitting yarn, cast on 8 sts and divide these sts between four of the needles, using the fifth to knit.
Round 1: k each st tbl.
Round 2: (yfwd, k1) 8 times (16 sts).
Rounds 3–5: knit.
Round 6: (yfwd, k1) 16 times (32 sts).
Rounds 7–11: knit.
Round 12: (yfwd, k1) 32 times (64 sts).
Rounds 13–19: knit.
Round 20: (yfwd, k2) 32 times (96 sts).
Round 21: knit.
Round 22: (yfwd, k6) 16 times (112 sts).
Round 23: knit.
Round 24: (yfwd, k7) 16 times (128 sts).
Round 25: knit.
Round 26: (yfwd, k8) 16 times (144 sts).
Round 27: knit.
Round 28: (yfwd, k2tog, k7) 16 times.
Round 29: knit.
Rep rounds 28 and 29 fourteen times more.
Round 58: knit.
Round 59: (k2tog, k7) 16 times (128 sts).
Rounds 60–66: knit.
Round 67: (k2, yfwd, k2tog) 32 times.
Rounds 68–73: knit.
Cast off, leaving a tail of yarn for sewing up.

Making up

Fold the brim to the inside along the row of eyelets and, using the tail of yarn, stitch the cast-on edge to the round at the base of the lacy pattern (round 59).

Blue Beauty

There is an eyelet row in the centre of the brim which, when the band is folded in half, creates an attractive border to the hat, with a double thickness to help keep its shape, and a picot edge.

Knit Knit Beanie

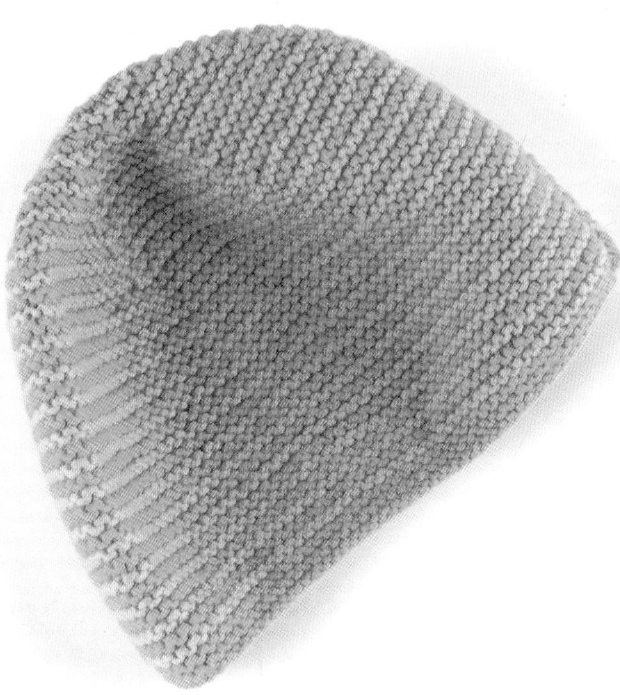

Materials:

2 x 50g balls double-knitting (8-ply) yarn (cotton blend) – lime green (A) turquoise blue (B)

Needles:

3mm (UK 11; US 3) knitting needles

3.75mm (UK 9; US 5) knitting needles

Tapestry needle

Tension:

23 sts and 24 rows to 10cm (4in), using 3.75mm (UK 9; US 5) knitting needles, measured over garter stitch.

Measurements and sizes:

To fit an average adult female head

Instructions:

Using 3mm needles and yarn B, cast on 112 sts.
Row 1: (k1, p1) to end.
Rep row 1 three times more.
Change to 3.75mm needles.
Rows 5 and 6: knit, using A; do not cut A but pick up B.
Rows 7 and 8: knit, using B; do not cut B but pick up A.
Rep rows 5–8 eight times more.
Row 41: (k13, k3tog) 7 times (98 sts).
Still changing colours after every alt row, work a further 9 rows.
Row 51: (k11, k3tog) 7 times (84 sts).
Still changing colours after every alt row, work a further 7 rows.
Row 59: (k9, k3tog) 7 times (70 sts).
Still changing colours after every alt row, work a further 5 rows.
Row 65: (k7, k3tog) 7 times (56 sts).
Still changing colours after every alt row, work a further 5 rows.
Row 71: (k5, k3tog) 7 times (42 sts).
Still changing colours after every alt row, work a further 3 rows.
Row 75: (k1, k2tog) 14 times (28 sts).
Knit 1 row.
Row 77: (k2tog) 14 times.
Knit 1 row.
Row 79: (k2tog) 7 times.
Cut yarn and thread tail through rem 7 sts.

Making up

With right sides together and using the tails of yarn, stitch up the back seam in backstitch; turn right sides out.

Soft Stripes

This simple garter stitch beanie also looks good made in nautical navy and cream stripes. Work the last 16–18 rows in plain cream, then make four navy pompoms, following the instructions on page 6, trim them to size with scissors, and then stitch them to the centre of the crown. This pattern is for an adult hat, but by working it in a 4-ply (fingering) yarn using 2.75mm (UK 12, US 2) and 3.25mm (UK 10, US 3) needles, you can produce a child-size version.

Bow Beanie

Materials:

2 x 50g balls double-knitting (8-ply) yarn (100% alpaca) – pink

Needles:

3.75mm (UK 9; US 5) knitting needles

Tapestry needle

Tension:

30 sts and 29 rows to 10cm (4in), measured over rib pattern, using 3.75mm (UK 9; US 5) knitting needles, (measured without stretching).

Measurements and sizes:

To fit an average adult female head

Instructions:

Band

Using 3.75mm needles and alpaca double-knitting yarn, cast on 30 sts.
Row 1 (WS): (p3, k3) 5 times.
Rep row 1 160 times.
Cast off, leaving 1 st on needle; do not cut the yarn.

Crown

With RS facing, pick up and knit 126 sts along the long edge of the band, inc. st. on needle.
Row 1 (WS): (p3, k3) 21 times.
Rep row 1 17 times.
Row 19: (p3, p2tog, p1) 21 times (105 sts).
Row 20: (p2, k3) 21 times.
Row 21: (p3,k2) 21 times.
Row 23: (p3, p2tog) 21 times (84 sts).
Row 24: (p1, k3) 21 times.
Row 25: (p3,k1) 21 times.
Row 26: (p1, k3) 21 times.
Row 27: (p3,k1) 21 times.
Row 28: k1, (sl1, k2tog, psso, k5) 10 times, sl1, k2tog, psso (62 sts).
Row 29: purl.
Row 30: k1, (sl1, k2tog, psso, k3) 10 times, p1 (42 sts).
Row 31: purl.
Row 32: k1, (sl1, k2tog, psso, k1) 10 times, p1 (22 sts).
Row 33: purl.
Row 34: k1, (k2tog) 10 times, k1 (12 sts).
Row 35: (p2tog) 6 times.
Cut yarn and thread tail through rem 6 sts.

Bow

Using 3.75mm needles and alpaca double-knitting yarn, cast on 21 sts.
Row 1 (RS): (k3, p3) 3 times, k3.
Row 2: (p3, k3) 3 times, p3.
Rep rows 1 and 2 48 times.
Cast off.

Centre

Cast on 6 sts.
Row 1 (RS): knit.
Row 2: purl.
Rep rows 1 and 2 24 times.
Cast off.

Making up

Pull up the tail of yarn to gather the stitches on top of the crown and secure then, with right sides together and using the tail of yarn, stitch up the seam in backstitch. On the band, pull up the stitches of the seam to gather the short ends together.
Stitch the short ends of the bow together, then wrap the centre piece around the join. Stitch the bow to the band, lining up the centre of the bow with the gathered part of the band.

Pretty in Pink

Alpaca yarn creates a really soft fabric that stretches beautifully – but you could substitute your own choice of yarn as long as it knits to the same tension.

Pigtails Beanie

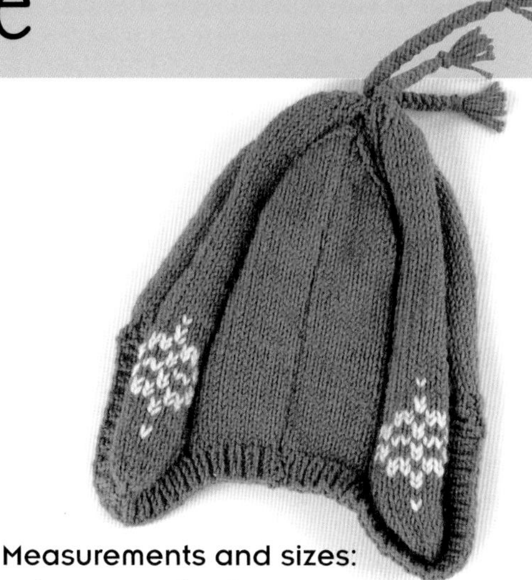

Materials:

2 x 50g balls aran (10-ply) yarn (merino, silk and cashmere blend) – pink

Small amount of aran (10-ply) yarn (merino, silk and cashmere blend) – ivory

Needles:

5mm (UK 6; US 8) knitting needles

Four 4mm (UK8; US6) double-pointed knitting needles

Tapestry needle

Tension:

19 sts and 27 rows to 10cm (4in), using 5mm (UK 6; US 8) knitting needles, measured over stocking stitch.

Measurements and sizes:

To fit an average female teen or adult head

Instructions:

Right ear flap

Using 5mm needles and aran yarn, cast on 9 sts.
Row 1: p1, k1, p1, k3, p1, k1, p1.
Row 2: k1, p1, k1, p3, k1, p1, k1.
Row 3: p1, k1, p1, m1, (k1, m1) 3 times, p1, k1, p1 (13 sts).
Row 4: k1, m1, p1, k2, p5, k2, p1, m1, k1 (15 sts).
Row 5: p2, k1, p2, k1, (m1, k1) 4 times, p2, k1, p2 (19 sts).
Row 6: k2, p1, k2, p9, k2, p1, k2.
Row 7: p2, k1, p2, k9, p2, k1, p2.
Rep rows 6 and 7 four times more.
Row 16: cast on 12 sts, p12, k2, p1, k2, p9, k2, p1, k2 (31 sts).
Row 17: p2, k1, p2, k9, p2, k1, p2, k to end.
Row 18: p12, k2, p1, k2, p9, k2, p1, k2.
Rep rows 17 and 18 four times more, then cut yarn and leave sts on a holder.

Left ear flap

Follow instructions for right ear flap to row 7, rep rows 6 and 7 three more times, rep row 6.
Row 15: cast on 12 sts, k12, p2, k1, p2, k9, p2, k1, p2 (31 sts).
Row 16: k2, p1, k2, p9, k2, p1, k2, p12.
Row 17: k12, p2, k1, p2, k9, p2, k1, p2.
Rep rows 16 and 17 four times more, then row 16 once more.
Next row: k12, p2, k1, p2, k9, p2, k1, p2, cast on 63 sts, then working from sts on holder for right ear flap, p2, k1, p2, k9, p2, k1, p2, k to end (125 sts).
Next row: p12, k2, p1, k2, p9, k2, p1, k2, p22, k2, p1, k2, p9, k2, p1, k2, p22, k2, p1, k2, p9, k2, p1, k2, p to end.
Next row: k12, p2, k1, p2, k9, p2, k1, p2, k22, p2, k1, p2, k9, p2, k1, p2, k22, p2, k1, p2, k9, p2, k1, p2, k to end.
Rep the last 2 rows 12 times more.

Crown shaping

Row 1: k10, k2tog, (k19, sl1, k1, psso, k18, k2tog) twice, k19, sl1, k1, psso, k to end (119 sts).
Row 2: purl.
Row 3: k9, k2tog, (k19, sl1, k1, psso, k16, k2tog) twice, k19, sl1, k1, psso, k to end (113 sts).
Row 4: purl.
Row 5: k8, k2tog, (k19, sl1, k1, psso, k14, k2tog) twice, k19, sl1, k1, psso, k to end (107 sts).
Row 6: purl.
Row 7: k7, k2tog, (k19, sl1, k1, psso, k12, k2tog) twice, k19, sl1, k1, psso, k to end (101 sts).
Row 8: purl.
Row 9: k6, k2tog, (k19, sl1, k1, psso, k10, k2tog) twice, k19, sl1, k1, psso, k to end (95 sts).

Row 10: p5, p2tog tbl, (k19, p2tog, p8, p2tog tbl) twice, k19, p2tog, p to end (89 sts).
Row 11: k4, k2tog, (k19, sl1, k1, psso, k6, k2tog) twice, k19, sl1, k1, psso, k to end (83 sts).
Row 12: p3, p2tog tbl, (k19, p2tog, p4, p2tog tbl) twice, k19, p2tog, p to end (77 sts).
Row 13: k2, k2tog, (k19, sl1, k1, psso, k2, k2tog) twice, k19, sl1, k1, psso, k to end (71 sts).
Row 14: p1, p2tog tbl, (k19, p2tog, p2tog tbl) twice, k19, p2tog, p to end (65 sts).
Row 15: k2tog, *k19, k2tog, rep from * twice more (61 sts).
Row 16: p3tog, p16, p3tog, p17, p3tog, p16, p3tog (53 sts)
Row 17: k2tog, k14, sl1,k1, psso, k7,sl1, k2tog, psso, k7, sl1, k1, psso, k14, k2tog, (47 sts)
Row 18: p2tog, (p3, p2tog) 9 times (37 sts)
Row 19: (k1, sl1, k2tog, psso) 9 times, k1 (19 sts)
Row 20: (p3tog) 6 times, p1.
Cut yarn and thread through rem 7 sts.

Cut yarn and thread tail through rem 22 sts.

Making up and border

Stitch up the back seam. With right sides facing and using two pairs of 4mm needles, starting at the centre back, pick up and knit 11 sts along the right back edge, 11 sts down the side of the ear flap, 3 sts from the cast-on edge of the ear flap, 18 sts up from the edge of the ear flap, 60 sts across front, 18 sts down the edge of the left ear flap, 3 sts along the cast-on edge of the ear flap, 11 sts up the back edge of the ear flap, 11 sts along the back edge to the centre (146 sts).
Round 1: (k1, p1) to end.
Round 2: (k1, p1) 11 times, k1 (p1, k1, p1) in next st, (k1, p1) 9 times, sl1, k2tog, psso, p1, (k1, p1) 28 times, sl1, k2tog, psso, (p1, k1) 9 times, (p1, k1, p1) in next st, (k1, p1) 11 times.
Round 3: (k1, p1) to end.
Round 4: (k1, p1) 12 times, (k1, p1, k1) in next st, (p1, k1) 9 times, p3tog, k1, (p1, k1) 27 times, p3tog, (k1, p1) 9 times, (k1, p1, k1) in next st, p1, (k1, p1) 11 times.
Round 5: (k1, p1) to end.
Cast off loosely in rib.

Swiss darning and plaits

Embroider the motifs on the ear flaps and front in Swiss darning, using ivory yarn and following the chart on page 7.
Make three plaits of varying lengths – 8cm (3¼in), 9cm (3½in) and 14cm (5½in) – each from 12 strands of pink yarn, and stitch to the top of the hat.

Classic Beanie

Materials:

2 x 50g balls aran (10-ply) yarn (100% wool tweed) – russet

Needles:

4mm (UK 8; US 6) knitting needles

5mm (UK 6; US 8) knitting needles

Tapestry needle

Tension:

16 sts and 23 rows to 10cm (4in), using 5mm (UK 6; US 8) knitting needles, measured over stocking stitch.

Measurements and sizes:

To fit an average adult male head

Instructions:

With 4mm needles and aran yarn, cast on 92 sts.
Row 1: (k2, p2) to end.
Rep row 1 15 times more.
Change to 5mm needles and, beg with a k row, work 24 rows in stocking stitch.
Row 51: (k13, k2tog) 6 times, k2 (86 sts).

Row 52 and each even-numbered (WS) row: purl.

Row 53: (k12, k2tog) 6 times, k2 (80 sts).

Row 55: (k11, k2tog) 6 times, k2 (74 sts).

Row 57: (k10, k2tog) 6 times, k2 (68 sts).

Row 59: (k9, k2tog) 6 times, k2 (62 sts).

Row 61: (k8, k2tog) 6 times, k2 (56 sts).

Row 63: (k7, k2tog) 6 times, k2 (50 sts).

Row 65: (k6, k2tog) 6 times, k2 (44 sts).

Row 67: (k5, k2tog) 6 times, k2 (38 sts).

Row 69: (k4, k2tog) 6 times, k2 (32 sts).

Row 71: (k3, k2tog) 6 times, k2 (26 sts).

Row 73: (k2, k2tog) 6times, k2 (20 sts)

Row 74: (p2tog) 10 times (10 sts).

Row 75: (k2tog) 5 times.

Cut yarn, leaving a tail, and thread through rem 5 sts.

Making up
Stitch up the back seam, reversing the seam on the ribbed band.

Mini Classic

For a child-size hat, follow the same pattern but use double-knitting (8-ply) yarn; you should need only one 50g ball. Cast on using 3.25mm (UK 10, US 3) needles and work 16 rows in rib, then change to 4mm (UK 8, US 6) needles before continuing. Check your tension: you should have 19 sts and 29 rows to 10cm (4in) using 4mm needles.

Baby Beanie

Materials:

1 50g ball double-knitting (8-ply) yarn – cream

Small amounts of double-knitting (8-ply) yarn in pale blue and pale pink

Needles:

3.25mm (UK 10; US 3) knitting needles

4mm (UK 8; US 6) knitting needles

3.25mm (UK 10; US 3) double-pointed knitting needles

Tapestry needle

Tension:

22 sts and 28 rows to 10cm (4in), using 4mm (UK 8; US 6) knitting needles, measured over stocking stitch.

Measurements and sizes:

In three sizes, to fit a baby aged approximately 9–12 (12–18; 18–24) months

Instructions:

Hat

Using 3.25mm double-pointed needles and double-knitting yarn, cast on 4 sts, cast off 2 sts, return st to left-hand needle; *cast on 3 sts, cast off 2 sts, return st to left-hand needle; rep from * until there are 81 (91; 101) sts.
Row 1: (k1, p1) to last st, k1.
Row 2: (p1, k1) to last st, p1.
Rep rows 1 and 2 five times more.
Row 13 (eyelet row): k2, (yfwd, k2tog) to last st, k1.
Row 14: (p1, k1) to last st, p1.
Row 15: (k1, p1) to last st, k1.
Rep rows 14 and 15 twice more then row 14 once more; change to 4mm needles.
Beg with a k row, work in stocking stitch until work measures 16 (17; 18) cm from eyelet row, ending with RS facing.

Shape crown

Row 1: k1, *k2tog, k8; rep from * to end of row; 73 (82; 91) sts.
Row 2 (and every WS row): p to end.
Row 3: k1, *k2tog, k7; rep from * to end; 65 (73; 81) sts.
Row 5: k1, *k2tog, k6; rep from * to end; 57 (64; 71) sts.
Row 7: k1, *k2tog, k5; rep from * to end; 49 (55; 61) sts.
Row 9: k1, *k2tog, k4; rep from * to end; 41 (46; 51) sts.
Row 11: k1, *k2tog, k3; rep from * to end; 33 (37; 41) sts.
Row 13: k1, *k2tog, k2; rep from * to end; 25 (28; 31) sts.
Row 15: k1, *k2tog, k1; rep from * to end.
Cut yarn and thread through rem 17 (19; 21) sts.

Cord (make two: one pink, one blue)

With 3.25mm double-pointed needles and pink or blue double-knitting yarn, cast on 2 sts.
Row 1: k2; do not turn but slide sts to other end of needle.
Rep this row until cord measures approximately 65cm long; cut yarn and fasten off.

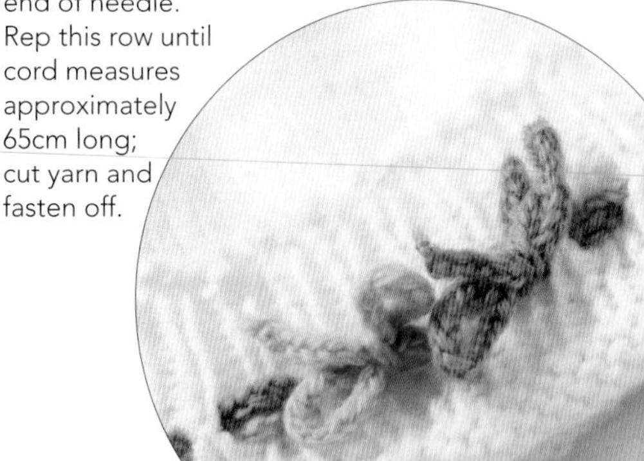

Making up

Stitch up the back seam. Thread the cords through the eyelets and tie the ends of each one in a neat bow.

Simply Gorgeous!

A special cast-on method creates a fancy edge on this simple hat that will suit any baby. Instructions are given for three different sizes. Thread knitted cords through the eyelet holes in the ribbed band, or leave them out and fold back the band along the eyelet row to create a picot effect.

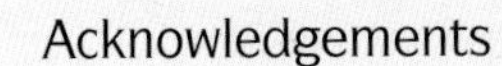

Acknowledgements

Thank you to everyone who has supplied me with yarns for use in making the projects for this book, including Patons, Rowan, King Cole, Sirdar, Sublime, Rico, Artesano and Designer Yarns (Debbie Bliss), and to Edith and Bill for trying on the hats while they were being developed. Thanks to Alison Shaw for her patience in managing the project and to Roz Dace for asking me to do the book in the first place.

Publisher's Note

If you would like more information about knitting, try the following books by Search Press:
Beginner's Guide to Knitting by Alison Dupernex, Search Press, 2004 and in the Twenty to Make series by Search Press: *Knitted Vegetables*, *Knitted Fruit*, and *Knitted Egg Cosies*,
all by Susie Johns, Search Press, 2011.
You are invited to visit the author's website:
www.susieatthecircus.typepad.com
Susie is also a member of the Ravelry online knitting community: www.ravelry.com